WRITTEN AND
ILLUSTRATED
BY
HEATHER NEUMANN

FOR THE
WORLD'S
LITTLE
HEROS

I know a secret

One I'm here to share

It's something you can use forever,

over here

or over there

I'm sure you've heard of super powers,

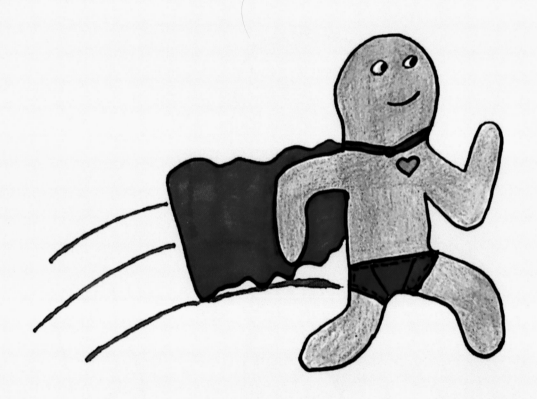

laser beams and super mega speed

But I bet you didn't know

theres only one superpower

any real hero needs

**Your hands may not have laser beams,
Or cut through things like razor seams...**

But they can change the world!

You can talk and you can listen,

You can lend a helping hand

You can speak up,

take a stand!

You can always say something nice,

or offer a friend some good advice!

Even though the world might not end

it sometimes feels that way
when you're in need of a friend

So make sure your words are kind

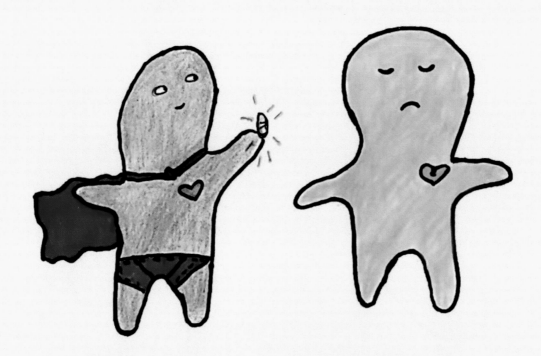

and your hands are gentle

Although you can't always feel it,

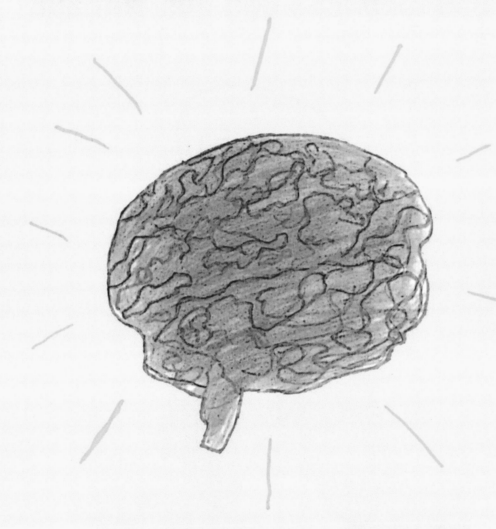

your powers are all mental

Use kindness and you will see

The superhero you will be

It's a super thing to be a friend,

you have crazy super powers
no need to pretend!

Sometimes the saving
someone may need

can be done with just
a simple good deed

So next time you wish
you could soar through the sky

Remember it's just as cool to say

before you say goodbye

Or bring someone a tissue

when they start to cry

So use kindness and you will see...

The superhero you will be!